POPULAR SONGS

CONTENTS

Beginning pitches on the CD are the root (tonic) of the song's key.

ISBN 978-1-4803-5233-9

HAL•LEONARD®
CORPORATION
7777 W. BLUEMOUND RD. P.O. BOX 13819 MILWAUKEE, WI 53213

Visit Hal Leonard Online at
www.halleonard.com

Ain't Misbehavin'

**Arrangement by EARL MOON
and ED WAESCHE**

Words by ANDY RAZAF
Music by THOMAS "FATS" WALLER and HARRY BROOKS

no one to walk with, but I'm hap-py on___ the shelf, ain't mis-be-hav-in',
ain't

I'm sav-in' my___ love for you,___ won-der-ful you.___ I know for cer-tain
And I

the one I love.___ I'm through with flirt-in', it's just you I'm think-in' of.

Ain't mis-be-hav-in', I'm sav-in' my___ love for you._____
Ain't
won-der-ful you._____

4

Like Jack Hor - ner   in the cor - ner,   don't go   no - where.
in ____   don't   go   no - where.

Like _____

What do I ___ care?   Your kiss - es   are   worth   wait - in'   for _____   be -

lieve ___   me. ___   I don't stay out late,   don't care to go. _____

And that's why   I

I'm home a - bout eight,   just   me and my ra - di - o.   Ain't mis - be - hav - in',

Ain't

Basin Street Blues

Arrangement by
DAVE BRINER

Words and Music by
SPENCER WILLIAMS

band's there to meet us,

New Or - leans.__ Ya know the band's there to meet us._____

band's there to meet us,

old friends to greet us.

old friends to greet us._____

old friends to greet us.

That's where the white__ an' the

black folks meet.__

Hea - ven on earth,__ they call it Ba - sin Street.__

Well

Chorus 1

Ba - sin Street__ is the street__ where the e - lite__ al - ways meet__ in

8

New Or - leans,____ land of dreams.____ You'll ne - ver know how nice it seems or

just how much it real - ly means.____ Glad to be,____ yes, sir - ee,____ where

wel - come's free,____ dear to me,____ where I can lose____ my Ba - sin Street

My

Verse 2

Well, well, I'm spread-in' the news.____ Ain't ya glad ya came with me?____

blues_____

Hallelujah

**Arrangement by
ADAM SCOTT**

**Words and Music by
LEONARD COHEN**

12

14

Chorus 3

From LES MISERABLES

Bring Him Home

**Arrangement by
RICH HASTY**

**Music by CLAUDE-MICHEL SCHÖNBERG
Lyrics by HERBERT KRETZMER and ALAIN BOUBLIL**

18

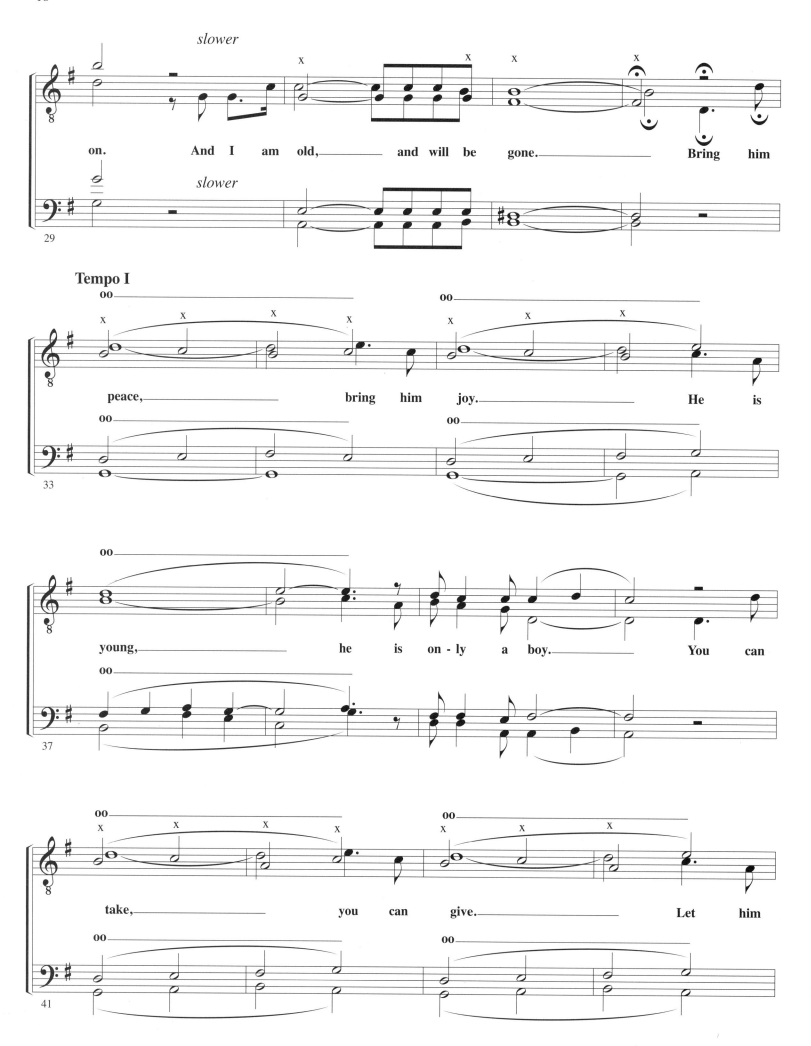

From Meredith Willson's THE MUSIC MAN

Seventy Six Trombones

Arrangement by the
BARBERSHOP HARMONY SOCIETY

By MEREDITH WILLSON

o - sos, the cream of ev - 'ry fam - ous band._____ Sev - en - ty -

six trom - bones caught the morn - ing sun,_____ with a hun - dred and ten cor -

nets right be - hind._____ There were more than a thou - sand reeds spring - ing

up like weeds, there were horns_____ of ev - 'ry shape and kind._____

ev - 'ry

ev - 'ry

Start-ing off with a big bang bong on a Chi - nese gong, by a

big bang bong - er at the rear._____ Sev - en - ty - six trom -

bones hit the coun - ter - point,_____ while a hun-dred and ten cor - nets played the

air._____ Then I mod - est - ly took my place as the one and on - ly

Tag

down the square.

bass, and I oom - pahed up and down the square. _____ Yes, I

down the square.

took my place as the one and on - ly bass, and I oom - pah

marched

oom - pah oom - pahed all a - round the square! _____

a - round, oom - pah oom - pah

oom - pah'd all a - round the square! _____

Stand By Me

**Arrangement by
STEVE DELEHANTY**

**Words and Music by JERRY LEIBER,
MIKE STOLLER and BEN E. KING**

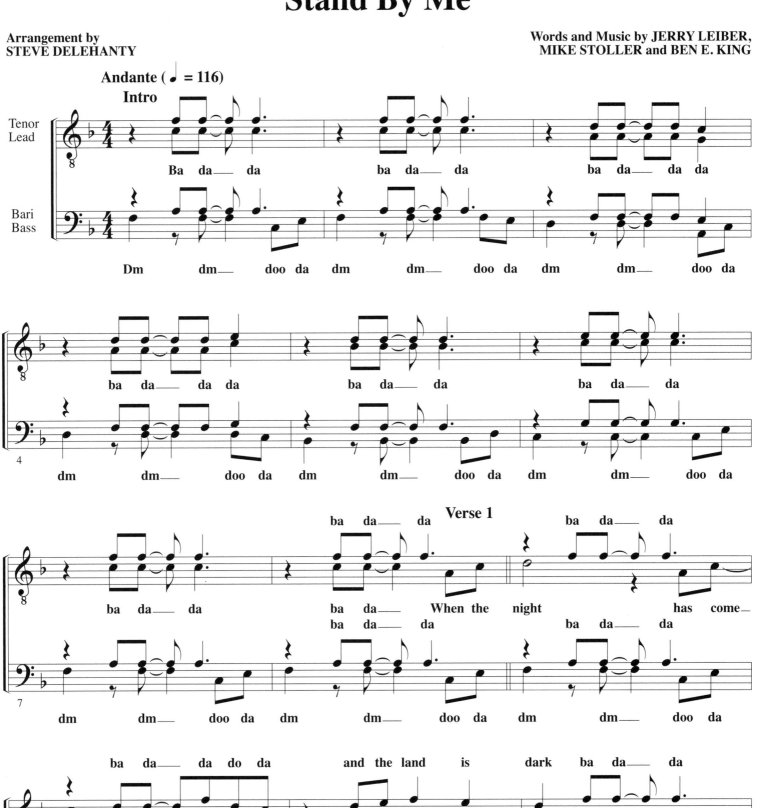

30

From Walt Disney Pictures' TOY STORY 2 - A Pixar Film

When She Loved Me

Arrangement by
JIM KAHLKE

Music and Lyrics by
RANDY NEWMAN

It's Only a Paper Moon

Arrangement by
CLAY HINE

Lyric by BILLY ROSE and E.Y. "YIP" HARBURG
Music by HAROLD ARLEN

Lead and tenor may wish to exchange parts here.